GW01607990

JERUSALEM
OF THE HEAVENS

Moshe Milner Yehuda Salomon

JERUSALEM

OF THE HEAVENS

THE ETERNAL CITY IN BIRD'S EYE VIEW

ALFA COMMUNICATION

Jerusalem of the Heavens

Moshe Milner Yehuda Salomon

General editor: Yehuda Schiff
Text: Danit Salomon
Translation: Henry G. Nijk

Air transportation: Chim-Nir, Nesher
Pilots: Yosi Barel (helicopter); Jacques Rubin and Avraham Vilan (light aircraft)
Colour Processing: Moris Kushelevitch
Development photographs:
Government Press Office; Orient Color
Typesetting: U.P.P. Ltd.
Colour separations and plates: Graphor Ltd.
Printing: Meiri Press Ltd
Binding: Peli Press Ltd.

Tel. 3-5794141 Fax. 3-5798977

The photographs in this book were taken with a Bronica GS-1 and Nikon cameras

ISBN 965-474-000-1

Introductory illustrations:

Acknowledgements

Our thanks to: Yosi Barel, our hawk-eyed helicopter pilot, whose maneuvering enabled us to capture every possible photographic angle; Jacques Rubin, who flew us through the night above the fireworks; Avraham Vilan, who shared our experience of freezing high above a snow-bedecked Jerusalem; Moris Kushelevitch, for his fast and efficient assistance; Moshe Calderon and his team at Graphor, for their professionalism and goodwill; Yaacov Sa'ar of the Government Press Office, who advised and assisted us throughout; Menahem Michelson, for his valuable advice; Wajeeh Nusseibeh, without whom we would not have been able to distinguish between the various religious denominations and rites; Mahmud Zaheikah, who helped to coordinate the photography of the worshippers at the Haram esh-Sharif; the Jerusalem Hilton, Sheraton-Plaza and Zion hotels, for enabling us to photograph from their roofs and for their hospitality; and to Hanan Nijk, the translator, who shared with us his knowledge and experience.

CONTENTS

A VIEW OF THE ANGELS

There are dozens, if not hundreds, of books with photographs of Jerusalem, which have not left one single spot unexplored — but all these photographs show the city from the perspective of the pedestrian. Sometimes he will descend into some cave or cistern, and every now and then he will climb upon a rooftop, but always his feet remain planted firmly upon the ground.

This means that one unique perspective remains hidden from his view: the earthly Jerusalem as seen from on high. Jerusalem as seen by an angel winging above the city, is the angle we have chosen to present the reader with a new and singular view of the city of Jerusalem.

For millions of people around the world the heavenly Jerusalem is a sacred symbol of their faith — faith in the revelation of a unified mankind at the End of Days. It has become a symbol which at times appears more real than the worldly Jerusalem below, and it is to this heavenly Jerusalem that their eyes are raised in hope and prayer.

In this book we have reversed the roles. Rather than focusing on the heavenly Jerusalem from below, we feature the earthly Jerusalem from above: the view of the birds, and the angels. From this perspective a different Jerusalem is revealed to us, unified, continuous, ancient and modern, sacred and profane. A city populated by Jews, Christians and Muslims in one harmonious whole. The camera reveals myriads of towers, turrets, domes and caves built side by side along slopes and valleys, literally as the Psalmist wrote: '... like a city that is built compactly together' (Ps. 122:3).

All the photographs in this book are taken from above — either from the air or from some elevated vantage point. They show us the entire city, from its earliest beginnings till the present day: markets, streets, alleyways, squares, parks, gardens, the palace of King David and the tomb of Jesus, synagogues, churches and mosques, domes of gold and of stone.

The photographs are taken from sunrise to sunset, during the day and at night, on workdays and festivals, during summer and winter, together blending into a picture of rare harmony.

★ ★ ★

Jerusalem, the city of David, is the centre of the world. Here the Jewish Temple was built, here Jesus was buried and from here Mohammed ascended to heaven.

The concept of a 'heavenly Jerusalem' has its origins in the heavenly sanctuary that appears in ancient Jewish legends. In these legends the heavenly Jerusalem was juxtaposed to the earthly Jerusalem, yet linked with it, as if to emphasize the affinity between our worldly and spiritual aspirations.

In later works, as well as in Christian literature, the distinction between the Temple of Jerusalem and the heavenly Jerusalem disappeared, and in its place the Scriptures tell us about a 'new Jerusalem coming down out of heaven', to take the place of the earthly Jerusalem (Revel. 21: 2).

For Jews, Jerusalem is the city of the God of Israel. Rabbi Eliezer said: 'Who prays in Jerusalem is as one praying before the throne of God, for the Gate of Heaven is there.' The divine promise of the eternity of the Kingdom of David and the eventual rebuilding of the Temple impart to the city an eternal holiness. The holiest places for the Jews are the Temple Mount and the Western Wall — the only remnant of the former Temple structure.

For Christians, Jerusalem derives its holiness from the events surrounding the final days on earth of Jesus — his passion, death and resurrection. Jesus was crucified and buried just outside the ancient city walls, to arise from his grave several days later and ascend to Heaven. Christianity's holiest places are therefore associated with the life and death of Jesus, in particular the Via Dolorosa and the Church of the Holy Sepulchre. In course of time many other sites, linked to the lives of persons close to Jesus also became sanctified.

The majority of Islamic holy places were so designated during the first decades following the Muslim conquest in the year 638 C.E. In this process both Jewish and Christian religious tradition played an important role. The most sacred site by far for Muslims is the *Es-Sakhra*, which Jewish tradition identified as the 'Foundation Stone' in the first Temple on Mount Moriah. The Muslims followed Jewish tradition in designating this spot as the 'centre of the world' and the place on which the world was founded. Above the *Es-Sakhra* the Muslims constructed the Dome of the Rock, and at the southern end of the former temple esplanade the Mosque of El-Aqsa, near the spot where according to Muslim tradition the prophet Mohammed ascended to heaven. Besides the Dome of the Rock the Muslims constructed many mosques and other religious buildings, which were similarly invested with sacred meanings.

All these events and shrines explain the unique experience that is called Jerusalem, and why three world religions regard the city as a centre of their world and 'a gate to the heavens'.

★ ★ ★

Jerusalem is situated on the eastern escarpment of the Judean hills, at the edge of the desert, surrounded by hills and valleys. This topographical situation, as well as the intermingling of old and new, impart to the city its remarkable colouration.

In the course of its 5000-year existence Jerusalem was passed from hand to hand. Its history is one long story of wars and conquests, which placed their stamp on both the physique and the character of the city. Historians tell us that Jerusalem was captured eighty-nine times. During the centuries it was ruled by Jebusites, Israelites, Babylonians, Persians, Greeks, Romans, Byzantines, Arabs, Ottoman Turks, Egyptians, Crusaders, Tatars, Mamluks, Mongols, Englishmen, Jordanians and — at present — Israelis.

Jerusalem is composed of two parts: the Old City, and the New City, that developed outside the city walls in the course of the last century. The city is divided into districts and neighbourhoods, which developed a distinctive character depending on the religion or ethnic or national origin of their inhabitants. By and large these distinctions are noticeable even today, although in many places the boundaries have begun to fade.

JERUSALEM CALENDAR

EARLY HISTORY until 1000 B.C.

First settlement. Jerusalem is already mentioned in ancient documents. It was ruled by an Amorite king called Adoni-Zedek. The city was temporarily occupied by the tribes of Judah and Benjamin, but they were unable to dislodge the Jebusites, who continued to populate the city.

FIRST TEMPLE PERIOD 1000 - 586 B.C.

1000 Conquest by King David
1000 - 922 Jerusalem capital of the united monarchy
960 King Solomon builds the Temple and a royal palace
701 Siege by the Assyrian king Sennacherib
598 Siege by the Babylonian king Nebuchadnezzar. King Jehoiachin and many of his subjects exiled to Babylon
586 Second siege by Nebuchadnezzar. The city is conquered and burned

SECOND TEMPLE PERIOD 536 B.C. - 70 A.D.

537 Declaration by king Cyrus. The return to Zion begins
516 Completion of the Second Temple
332 Capture of Jerusalem by Alexander the Great
168 Antiochus IV Epiphanes occupies the city
164 Jerusalem occupied by Judah Maccabee
164 - 37 The Hasmonean period
37 - 4 Herod captures the city
4 B.C. - 41 A.D. Judea ruled by Roman procurators
34 A.D. Crucifixion of Jesus
41 - 44 Rule of Herod Agrippa
66 - 70 The Jewish Revolt
70 Titus captures Jerusalem. His troops raze the city and set fire to its houses and the Second Temple

AELIA CAPITOLINA 135 - 324

131 - 135 Bar Kokhba Rebellion against Roman rule
135 The Emperor Hadrian rebuilds Jerusalem as a Roman city and names it "Aelia Capitolina". A temple to Jupiter is erected on the Temple Mount and Jews are forbidden entrance to the city

BYZANTINE PERIOD 326 - 638

324 Rule of the emperor Constantine. Erection Church of the Holy Sepulchre and a new wall surrounding Mount Zion
361 - 363 Emperor Julian "the Apostate" permits Jews to settle in the city
525 - 565 Rule of the emperor Justinian. Construction of the Cardo, the "Nea" basilica and other Christian sites
614 - 629 Persian conquest of the city
629 - 638 Byzantine reconquest of Jerusalem

EARLY ARAB PERIOD 638 - 1099

638 Conquest of Jerusalem by the Arabs under the caliph Omar
638 - 650 Umayyad rule. Reconstruction of the Temple Mount. Erection of the Dome of the Rock, the el-Aqsa mosque and other Muslim buildings. Jewish resettlement of Jerusalem

750 - 969 Abbasid rule.
969 - 1071 Fatimid rule
1012 Destruction of the Church of the Holy Sepulchre
1071 Conquest by the Turkish Seljuks
1096 Egyptian conquest

FIRST CRUSADER PERIOD 1099 - 1187

1099 Capture of Jerusalem by the Crusaders. Massacre of the Muslim and Jewish inhabitants. Jews are forbidden to live in the city
1099 - 1187 Rebuilding of the Holy Sepulchre and other churches

AYYUBID PERIOD 1187 - 1267

1187 Saladin conquers the city and permits the Jews to return
1229 - 1244 Second Crusader period
1244 Conquest by the Khwarizm (Tartar) Turks
1260 Mongol conquest and destruction of the city

MAMLUK PERIOD 1267 - 1517

1267 Mamluk conquest. Nahmanides (the Ramban) persuades Jews to return to Jerusalem
1400 Jews begin to settle the "Jewish Quarter". Erection of the Ramban synagoque
1488 Brief Mongol conquest accompanied by widespread destruction

OTTOMAN PERIOD 1517 - 1917

1517 Conquest by the Ottoman Turks
1538 - 1542 Construction of the new city wall
1721 Muslims seize the quarter of the Eastern-European ("Ashkenazi") Jews and burn their synagogue
1812 Ashkenazi Jews begin to return to Jerusalem
1854 First residential buildings outside the Old City
1873 Building of the German Colony by the Templars
1877 Establishment "municipal council" in Jerusalem
1892 Inauguration of the railway connecting Jaffa and Jerusalem
1914 - 1917 First World War in Palestine

THE BRITISH MANDATE 1917 - 1948

1917 General Allenby captures the city
1925 Inauguration of the Hebrew University on Mount Scopus
1928 - 1938 Headquarters of Jewish national institutions established in Jerusalem
1948 Israeli War of Independence. The Jewish Quarter falls into Jordanian hands. Division of the city under Israeli and Jordanian rule

A DIVIDED CITY 1948 - 1967

Jerusalem remains divided under Israeli and Jordanian rule
1949 - 1967 Construction of the Kirya Government district, the Knesset and the Israel Museum in western Jerusalem

JERUSALEM REUNITED from 1967

1967 The Six-day War. Reunification of both parts of the city under Israeli rule.

 ◇ The Western Wall

◇ Ceremony of the opening of the doors to the Holy Sepulchre ▷

THE FIRST GATE

A house of prayer for all nations

(Isaiah 56:7)

There will come a time in which all nations and all dominions will assemble in Jerusalem, for it is said: "...and all nations will gather in Jerusalem to honour the name of the Lord." (Jeremiah 3:17)

(Sayings of Rabbi Nathan, 35)

 ◇ Jews hurrying to their prayers at the Western Wall

◇ Muslim returning from prayers at the Haram esh-Sharif

◇ A Muslim fingers his prayer beads

◇ **Bind them on your fingers...** (Proverbs 7:3)

Two aspects of the Wall
◇ The esplanade in front of the Western Wall and the Haram esh-Sharif ▷

Pages 27-28 overleaf: ◇ Jewish pilgrims at the Western Wall
Pages 29-30 overleaf: ◇ Muslims on the Haram esh-Sharif

◇ Muslims kneeling at prayer on the Haram esh-Sharif

◇ Jews at the Western Wall. The Blessing of the Priests at the Feast of Tabernacles

 Worshippers at the Western Wall ◇ The men's section

◇ The women's section

The man who enters by the gate is the shepherd of his sheep (John 10: 2)
◇ The Latin Patriarch at the entrance to the Holy Sepulchre

... and his sheep follow him (John 10:4)
◇ The procession of the Greek-Orthodox Patriarch leaves the Holy Sepulchre

◇ Greek-Orthodox pilgrims during the Palm Sunday services at the Holy Sepulchre

◇ Jews reading the Torah

◇ Yeshiva student

◇ Muslim

◇ The Latin Patriarch

◇ Franciscan monk

◇ Hadj in the el-Aqsa mosque

The Choir ◇ The Latin choir in the Holy Sepulchre ▷

 ...a woman who fears the Lord (Proverbs 31:30) ◇ Ethiopian prayer book written in the Ghez language

◇ Jewish women at the tomb of Rabbi Simon the Just

◇ Christian pilgrims in the Via Dolorosa

◇ Ethiopian pilgrim women

◇ Greek pilgrim women

...sit on the ground without a throne (Isaiah 47:1)
◇ Muslim women at prayer on the Haram esh-Sharif

◇ A pilgrim climbs upon the roof

◇ Observing from on high

◇ Walking in the square

◇ Lighting candles at the Omphalos

...ten virgins who took their lamps and went out to meet the bridegroom (Matth. 25:1)
◇ Catholic pilgrims dressed as brides during the Palm Sunday procession

 ◇ Ultra-Orthodox Jews accompany the Admor of Gur on his final journey

One was to proceed on top of the wall to the right (Nehemiah 12:31) ◇ Festive procession around the walls on Jerusalem Day ▷

... marched out of the city (I Kings 20:19) ◇ Muslims passing through the Lion's Gate at the conclusion of their Friday prayers

◁ **...men coming from the direction of the upper gate** (Ezekiel 9:2)
◇ Roman-Catholics pilgrims emerging from the Lion's Gate during the Palm Sunday procession

The four species ◇ Jewish worshippers at the Western Wall during the Feast of Tabernacles

"Hosanna!" (Matth. 21:9) ◇ Syrian Orthodox Jacobites praying in the Church of the Holy Sepulchre on Palm Sunday

◇ Muslim washing his feet at the el-Kas

◇ Armenian-Catholic ceremony

◇ Roman-Catholic ceremony

◇ Ethiopian ceremony

◇ Greek-Orthodox ceremony

...and began to wash his disciples' feet (John 13:5) ◇ The ritual Washing of the Feet

◇ The Greek-Orthodox Footwashing Ceremony ▷

◇ The Roman-Catholic Procession of the Cross

Carrying his own cross... (John 19:17)

◇ Greek-Orthodox pilgrims cross themselves at the conclusion of the procession ▷

◇ The Procession of the Cross in historical dress

◇ Yeshiva student in Purim dress

◇ The Latin Patriarch lighting the flame

◇ The flame is carried in the Greek-Orthodox ceremony

◇ Candle lighting during the Roman-Catholic ceremony

◇ The lights of Jerusalem at night

The miracle of the lights ◇ Lighting a Jerusalem Hanukkah lamp

◇ The chandelier in the dome of the Catholicon

◇ Fireworks above the Old City

 Lag Be'omer celebration at the tomb of Rabbi Simon the Just ◇ The "halake" ceremony

◇ Celebrants in a festive dance

◇ Street dancers during the launch of Jerusalem Year

◇ Shabiyat cakes ▷

THE SECOND GATE

From the streets of Jerusalem...

(Jeremiah 7:34).

Once again men and women of ripe old age will sit in the streets of Jerusalem, each with cane in hand because of his age. The city streets will be filled with boys and girls playing there.

(Zechariah 8:4-5)

◇ The Cardo

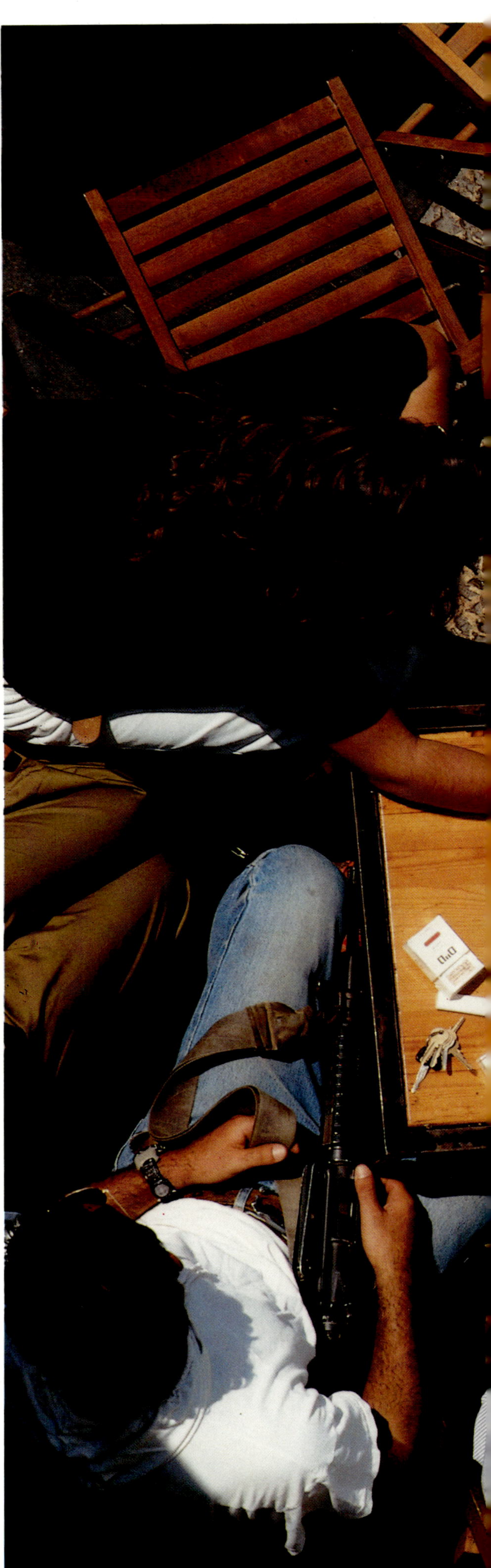

◇ Lounging in the Ben-Yehuda Mall

◇ The Ben-Yehuda Mall at night ▷

BIG apple pizza
anchovie

 Spread out above the heads... (Ezekiel 1:22) ◇ Scenes in Market Street

◇ Customer carrying her purchases

 ◇ Market at Damascus Gate Square

◇ Market scene

◇ Market stall at Damascus Gate Street ▷

KENT

KENT

◇ Easter eggs

מונקו

◇ Corner in an Old City courtyard

◇ Seats of the Teddy Stadium

... they encamp, each in his own place (Num. 2:17) ◇ Parking lot near the Damascus Gate ▷

◇ A quiet camping place at the Jaffa Gate

◇ Hilton Hotel parking lot at night

◇ Jewish summer camp closing ceremony at the Western Wall ▷

POLICE

◇ Roof of the Bible Lands Museum ▷

THE THIRD GATE

Stones and lights

...I will build you with stones of turquoise,
your foundations with sapphires.
I will make your battlements of rubies,
your gates of sparkling rubies,
and all your walls of precious stones.

(Isaiah 54:11-12)

◇ Dawn

◇ High noon

◇ Twilight

◇ Night

◇ Zion Gate

◇ Dung Gate

◇ Golden Gate

◇ Entrance gate to "City Wall apartments" in Gilo

◇ Jaffa Gate

◇ The Monastery of the Cross

◇ In the Eleona

◇ The Augusta Victoria hospital

◇ The towers at the entrance

Notre Dame de France

◇ General view

◇ The bell tower of St. George's cathedral

◇ Minaret of the Sons of A'wanima mosque

◇ Spice box

◇ Bell tower of the Mar Zakariya church

◇ Church of the Visitation

◁ ◇ Church of the Redeemer

◇ Mount Scopus and the Hebrew University in the snow

◇ Hebrew Union College

◇ The museum in the snow

◇ The museum at sunrise ▷

◇ The Rockefeller Museum

◇ View from the west

◇ View from the east ▷

◇ The octagonal roof of the church

The Italian hospital

◁ ◇ The hospital; behind it the Department of Education building

◇ The Haram esh-Sharif at night

◇ The Abyssinian Church

◇ Dome of the Rock

◇ Sabil Qaitbay

◇ "Yeled tov Jerushala'im" ("A good Jerusalem boy")

◇ Church of the Holy Sepulchre. Domes of the rotunda and the Catholicon

◇ Church of the Sisters of the Rosary convent

◇ St. Peter in Gallicantu church

◇ The Florence Dworsky Conservatory

◇ The Dominus Flevit church

... the tombs that were there on the hillside (2 Kings 23:2) ◇ The Jewish cemetery on the Mount of Olives

◁ **Mount of Olives** ◇ View from the east

◇ Absalom's Tomb

◇ Golden cupolas of the Church of Mary Magdalene ▷

 The Russian Cathedral ◇ General view

◇ The green domes

◇ The cathedral in the snow

David's Tomb ◇ Mount Zion

5

 ◇ Mount Zion hotel

On the steps of the rock

◇ Haceldama monastery ▷

◇ The Palace building

Terra Sancta college ◇ By day and at night

◇ Reflections in the windows of the Hyatt hotel

◇ Sheraton-Plaza hotel

◇ Kennedy Memorial

◁ ◇ The Jerusalem Theatre. The Henry Crown Concert Hall

◇ The Jewish Quarter and the Temple Mount in the snow ▷

◇ A rosy sunrise above the Old City

◁ ◇ Dawn above the Jewish Quarter

He wraps himself in light as with a garment (Psalms 104:2)

◇ The Christian Quarter bathed in sunshine

◇ Coral sunset on the Zichron Yosef Quarter ▷

...the houses in Jerusalem (Isaiah 22: 10)

◇ Yemin Moshe Quarter

◇ In Ramot Polin Quarter

◇ Tin-clad walls in Mahane Yehuda Quarter ▷

סימה
SIMMA
RESTAURANT & STEAK
משקאות חיים
משקאות
חיים
משקאות חיים
Coca-Cola

◇ Laromme hotel

◇ The convent of the Franciscan Sisters

 ◇ Silwan (Kfar Shiloah)

◇ The Gilo Quarter ▷

◇ Haas Promenade

◁ **...the stairs that go down** (Nehemiah 3:15) ◇ Stairway in Yemin Moshe

◇ The Garden of Gethsemane and the Church of All Nations

 ...there was a garden, and in the garden a new tomb (John 19:41) ◇ The Garden Tomb

◇ Sherover Promenade

◇ The Bethesda Pool (Sheep Pool)

◇ The Swimming pool of the American Colony hotel

◇ The Jerusalem Pool

◇ The Mamilla Pool in the snow

◁ **the King's Pool** (Nehemiah 2:14) ◇ The swimming pool of the King David Hotel

◇ Hechal Shelomo

◇ The Knesset covered in snow ▷

◇ The Jewish Quarter

◇ Section of the excavations at the Western Wall

◇ Section of the Jewish Quarter ▷

 ◇ The Archeological Garden and the rebuilt Jewish Quarter

...they dwell in Jerusalem forever (1 Chron. 23:25)

◇ Remnants of the Ummayad palace and the el-Aqsa mosque ▷

◇ Roof of the President's residence

◇ Baklava cakes

◇ Swimming pool at the Laromme hotel

◇ Patio at the Hilton hotel

◇ Honeycomb apartments at Ramot Polin

◇ "Center 1" Shopping Mall

◇ Welcome !

◇ Farewell !

BEHIND THE PHOTOGRAPHS

2-3 **The Old City at sunrise —** The Old City forms the eastern part of Jerusalem, bordered by the Kidron Valley to the east and the Hinnom Valley to the south and west. The city is a dense warren of buildings and alleyways at various levels, the earliest dating back thousands of years. The dominant construction style is Arabic. The Temple Mount, situated in the south-eastern part, occupies about one-fifth of the Old City area. It forms a distinct part of the city, and is separated from it by a wall.
The Old City is enclosed by a 4-km long wall, constructed on the remnants of earlier walls. From it project 45 watchtowers, the largest being the Citadel tower, better known as David's Tower. The city can be entered through seven gates: the Damascus Gate, Herod's Gate (Flower Gate), Lion's Gate (St. Stephen's Gate), Dung Gate, Zion Gate, Jaffa Gate and the New Gate.
The Old City and its vicinity contain countless historical places and sites holy to three religions. Various ethnic-religious groups settled in the city around their respective holy sites, resulting in its present division into four quarters:
The Muslim quarter is the largest of the four. It occupies the south-eastern part of the Old City, adjoining the Temple Mount (to Muslims: *Haram esh-Sharif*) and the Dome of the Rock. Here are concentrated most of the mosques and Muslim religious institutions, as well as the seat of the Muslim religious trust (*Waqf*).
The Christian quarter is situated in the north-western corner, around the Church of the Holy Sepulchre. In this quarter are the seats of the various Patriarchates, as well as a large number of churches and monasteries. The Christian institutions extend into the Muslim quarter along the Via Dolorosa.
The Armenian quarter is situated in the south-western part, around the Church of St. James and the adjoining Armenian Patriarchate, which in turn is contained within a wall.
The Jewish quarter, finally, occupies the south-eastern part of the Old City, close to the Western Wall. (see 20)

4-5 **The Old City as seen from the west.**

6-7 **The city covered in snow, as seen from the south-east.**

8-9 **Ultra-orthodox Jews at Shabbat Square —** Demonstration by ultra-orthodox Jews against Shabbat desecration by secular citizens.

12-13 **Christians in the square before the Holy Sepulchre.** (see 38)

16-17 **Muslims at prayer on the Temple Mount —** Haram esh-Sharif (the "Temple Mount" to Jews), built on the top of Mount Moriah, is encircled by walls: to the south-east and east by the Old City walls, and on the remaining sides by an inner retaining wall which separates it from the Old City. The plateau of the Haram esh-Sharif has two levels — an esplanade and a raised central section. This central plateau is reached by ascending eight steps, topped by a series of archways. At the centre of the plateau rises the Dome of the Rock, built above the *Es-Sakhra* ("Foundation stone"), and at the southern end the el-Aqsa mosque. The esplanade contains still other structures, built in the course of the centuries. The Haram esh-Sharif is maintained by the *Waqf,* the Muslim religious trust. (see also 29, 42)

18-19 **Fireworks display above the Old City —** One of the events during Jerusalem Year. The 25th anniversary of the unification of the two parts of the city was proclaimed Jerusalem Year. Photographed from an airplane flying above the fireworks.

20 **The Western Wall** — The holiest site of the Jews. It is a part of the retaining wall of the Second Temple that remained intact following the destruction of the sanctuary. Succeeding generations of Jews have come here to pray and lament the destruction of the Temple.
The wall is constructed of hewn blocks of stone, the lower courses of which date from the time of Herod. Between the war of 1948 and the Six-Day War Jews were not allowed access to the wall. Following the Six-Day War the area between the Jewish Quarter and the wall was cleared and a large plaza constructed.

21 **Ceremony of the opening of the doors to the Holy Sepulchre —** Ever since the fall of the Crusader kingdom Muslims have held the keys to the church. For many generations now they have been in safekeeping with the Nusseibeh family, and even today the doors are opened by one of the members of this family. The photograph shows Wajeeh Nusseibeh climbing a ladder to open the two round locks with the ancient key.

22 **Jews hurrying to their prayers at the Western Wall.** (see 20)

23 **Muslim returning from prayers at the Haram esh-Sharif.** (see 16)

24 **A Muslim fingers his prayer beads.**

25 **Bind them on your fingers... —** An ultra-orthodox "hassidic" Jew attempts to unravel a knot in his silk belt.

26+31 **The esplanade in front of the Western Wall and the Haram esh-Sharif.** (see 16, 20)

27-28 **Jewish pilgrims at the Western Wall** — Prayers during the Feast of Tabernacles. During the Feast of Tabernacles (*Succot*) thousands of Jews come to pray at the Western Wall. Succot, which falls on the 15th of Tishri, is one of the three traditional pilgrimage festivals which Jews used to celebrate in Jerusalem. "Live in booths for seven days... so that your descendants will know that I made the Israelites live in booths when I brought them out of Egypt." (Levit. 23:42-43) Even today Jews build such booths during Succot, in which they eat and even sleep. (see also 56)

29-30 **Muslims on the Haram esh-Sharif —** Friday prayers during the month of Ramadan. Ramadan is the name of the ninth month in the Muslim calendar. Fasting, as practiced during the month of Ramadan, is fourth among the five most important religious commandments of Islam. During the month of Ramadan Muslims are expected to abstain from eating, drinking, smoking, cosmetics and sexual relations from sunset till sundown. Once the sun has set, they may eat and drink and conduct their lives as usual till morning.

32 **Muslims kneeling at prayer on the Haram esh-Sharif** — Prayer is one of the five main religious commandments of Islam. The Muslim prays five times a day, at specific hours, kneeling on a small prayer rug, with his face turned to the city of Mecca. (see also 16)

33 **Jews at the Western Wall. The Blessing of the Priests at the Feast of Tabernacles** — The source of the priestly blessing is found in the book of Numbers, where the *cohanim,* the descendants of Aharon are commanded to bless the Israelites each and every day, an obligation which still exists today. For the blessing the cohanim ascend the dais and face the Holy Ark, after having first removed any

leather footwear. Then, turning to face the congregation, they repeat the traditional priestly blessing after the hazan. While pronouncing the blessing the cohanim keep their arms raised towards the congregation, who avoid looking at the cohanim but keep their eyes turned down to their prayer books.

34-35 **Worshippers at the Western Wall. The men's section and the women's section** — As is customary in synagogues, separate sections have been allocated to male and female worshippers at the Western Wall.

36-37 **The Old City**

38 **The Latin Patriarch at the entrance to the Holy Sepulchre** — The Church of the Holy Sepulchre is Christianity's holiest site in Jerusalem. On this spot Jesus was crucified and buried, and here he arose from the dead. The first church on this site was erected in the 4th century by the emperor Constantine and his mother Helena. In the year 614 the Persians conquered Jerusalem, and they burned and razed the church. In 628 the city was captured by the Byzantine emperor Heraclius, who rebuilt the church. The church was once again destroyed in 1009 by the Fatimid caliph El-Hakim (only the actual tomb and the structure above the rock of Golgotha were left standing), after which a new church was built between 1042-1048 in the days of the emperor Monomachus. The present church, which was built by the Crusaders and dedicated in 1149, contains parts of the church of Monomachus.
Inside the church are the five last Stations of the Cross, namely: tenth station, where Jesus was stripped of his garments; eleventh station, where Jesus was nailed to the cross; twelfth station, the spot where the cross was raised; thirteenth station, the place where Mary sat next to her crucified son; fourteenth and last and most sacred station, where Jesus was placed in the sepulchre. (see also 62)
The church is in the hands of mainly three denominations: the Greek-Orthodox, the Roman-Catholics and the Armenians. Several smaller sections of the edifice are held by the Copts and the Syrian Jacobites, while an even smaller part outside the actual building (the Dir el-Sultan) is in the hands of the Ethiopian Church. The status quo between the various Churches was determined during the Ottoman era and ratified during the British mandatory period.

39 **The procession of the Greek-Orthodox Patriarch leaves the Holy Sepulchre.**

40 **Greek-Orthodox pilgrims during the Palm Sunday service at the Holy Sepulchre** — At the bottom of the photograph is the stone on which it is said Jesus' body was laid out and prepared for burial. The rectangular stone slab is on three sides surrounded by candlesticks, respectively of the Franciscans, Greek-Orthodox and Armenians. (see 54)

41 **Jews reading the Torah** — Eastern-European (*Ashkenazi*) Jews read the Torah in front of the Western Wall.

42 **Yeshiva student; Muslim; the Latin Patriarch; Franciscan monk** — engrossed in reading the Scriptures.

43 **Hadj in the el-Aqsa mosque** — El-Aqsa on the Haram esh-Sharif is the oldest mosque in the Holy land and one of the largest and most important in the world. The first mosque on this site was a wooden structure erected by the caliph Omar following his arrival in Jerusalem in the year 638. In 705 the Ummayad caliph el-Walid erected a large stone building in its place. It was destroyed during an earthquake in 747, rebuilt, and destroyed once again in the year 1033. In 1035 the building was redesigned, and the present dome and entrance gates put in place.
The Crusaders turned the mosque into a palace for the Crusader kings and, after several renovations, called it "The Temple of Solomon". Eventually the palace became the headquarters of the Order of the Templars. When Saladin took Jerusalem from the Crusaders in 1187, the building once more became a mosque.
During the present century el-Aqsa was twice struck by earthquakes (in 1927 and 1936), necessitating fundamental repairs. In 1969 a deranged Australian tourist set fire to the mosque, causing considerable damage. In the wake of this fire, further extensive repairs were undertaken.
A Hadj is a Muslim who has observed the commandment of the pilgrimage to Mecca.

44-45 **The Latin choir in the Holy Sepulchre** — Latin mass during the Ceremony of the Holy Fire. (see 66)

46 **Ethiopian prayer book written in the Ghez language** — Ethiopian pilgrim praying at the Dir el-Sultan. (see 59)

47 **Jewish women at the tomb of Rabbi Simon the Just** — According to an ancient tradition Simon the Just, one of the High Priests in the Temple who lived at the end of the 4th or the 3rd century B.C., was buried in this cave.
Christian pilgrims in the Via Dolorosa — Pilgrims studying the route of the Via Dolorosa in their guide book.

48 **Ethiopian pilgrim women; Greek pilgrim women** — A brief pause between rituals.

49 **Muslim women at prayer on the Haram esh-Sharif** — As is customary among Jews, Muslim women pray separately from the men. (see also 16)

50 **A pilgrim climbs upon the roof; Observing from on high; Walking in the square** — At Easter time thousands of Greek-Orthodox pilgrim women from Greece and Cyprus come to visit Jerusalem. Many are dressed in black, and carry a small folding stool which enables them to rest while waiting for the next religious event. No effort is too great for them to watch the rites in the plaza of the Church of the Holy Sepulchre, even if this means climbing on an adjoining roof.
Lighting candles at the Omphalos — The Omphalos is a stone in the Catholicon of the Church of the Holy Sepulchre. According to Christian tradition this is the centre of the world.

51 **Catholic pilgrims dressed as brides during the Palm Sunday procession**. (see 54)

52 **Ultra-orthodox Jews accompany the Admor of Gur on his final journey** — Thousands of mourners accompanied the funeral procession of Rabbi Simcha Bunim Alter, the Admor of Gur, who died on June 9, 1992.

53 **Festive procession around the walls on Jerusalem Day.** (see 18)

54 **Roman-Catholic pilgrims emerging from the Lion's Gate during the Palm Sunday procession** — The rites of Palm Sunday are the most important in the Roman-Catholic religious year. The celebrations take place on the Sunday preceding Easter (following the Gregorian calendar).
According to the New Testament Jesus rode from Bethphage to Jerusalem on a donkey: "They brought the donkey and the colt, placed their cloaks on them, and Jesus sat on them. A very large crowd spread their cloaks on the road, while others cut branches from the trees and spread them on the road. The crowds that went ahead of him and those that followed shouted: 'Hosanna to the Son of David! Blessed is he who comes in the name of the Lord! Hosanna in the highest!'" (Matth. 21:7-9).
On Palm Sunday Jesus' entry is commemorated with a procession that starts at Bethphage and enters the city through the Lion's Gate, continuing along the Via Dolorosa. The celebrants carry palm branches (called "Hosanna") and olive branches, while chanting "Hosanna, Hosanna".

55 **Muslims passing through the Lion's Gate at the conclusion of their Friday prayers** — The Lion's Gate, which forms part of the eastern section of the Turkish wall, is so

called because of the two lions (in fact panthers) above the gate. The gate was built by Suleiman the Magnificent in the year 1538.

56 **Jews worshipping at the Western Wall during the Feast of Tabernacles** — One of the principal commandments of the Succot festival is that of the Four Species: "On the first day you are to take choice fruit from the trees, and palm fronds, and boughs of thick trees, and willows of the brook, and you shall rejoice before the Lord your God..." (Levit. 23:40). The plants chosen to represent the four species are the ethrog (of the citrus family), a palm branch, a twig of myrtle (bough of a thick tree) and a willow branch. During the morning service of Succot the worshippers keep the Four Species in their hand. (see also 27)

57 **Syrian Orthodox Jacobites praying in the Church of the Holy Sepulchre on Palm Sunday.** (see 54)

58 **Muslim washing his feet at the el-Kas** — The el-Kas is a circular stone basin on the Haram esh-Sharif where Muslims wash their face, hands and feet prior to commencing their prayers. It is surrounded by a wrought-iron railing, with at the centre a stone fountain in the shape of a vase. Around the perimeter are a number of taps. The fountain was built in 1320; the mosaic at the centre and the taps were added during the Ottoman period.

59 **The ritual Washing of the Feet** — "And it was just before the Passover Feast... so he got up from the meal, took off his outer clothing, and wrapped a towel around his waist. After that, he poured water into a basin and began to wash his disciples' feet, drying them with the towel that was wrapped around him." (John 13:1, 4-5) Each year before Easter the Christians re-enact the footwashing ceremony. The highest prelate of each Church washes the feet of a dozen members of the lower clergy. The Roman-Catholic date is determined according to the Gregorian calendar, while the ceremonies of the Eastern Churches follow the Julian calendar.
The Armenian Catholic ceremony — This ceremony is held in the Polish church, which is presently in the possession of the Armenian Catholics. The photograph shows the Archbishop washing the feet of a dozen children.
The Roman-Catholic ceremony — The Latin Patriarch washes the feet of six novices. At the end of the ceremony each of them receives a small silver crucifix.
The Ethiopian ceremony — The Ethiopian footwashing ceremony takes place at the Dir el-Sultan (the Ethiopian courtyard situated on the roof of St. Helena's Chapel of the Holy Sepulchre). The ceremony is held inside a large tent specially erected for the Passover. After the Archbishop and the twelve chosen candidates for the foot-washing have made seven circuits inside the tent, the Archbishop takes off his splendid mantle and crown, dons a white gown and rubs the feet of the twelve candidates with water and vine leaves.
The Greek-Orthodox ceremony — This is the most impressive of the various footwashing ceremonies, conducted on a podium erected for this purpose in the plaza before the entrance of the Church of the Holy Sepulchre. During the ceremony the plaza and surrounding balconies and roofs are packed with a dense throng. On each side of the podium are seated half a dozen members of the lower clergy, with the Patriarch in the middle. Two assistants divest the Patriarch of his ceremonial robe and his resplendent crown, after which they wrap him in a white gown. The Patriarch bends down and washes, and after this wipes, a foot of each of those sitting before him. When all of them have had their feet washed, the Patriarch rinses his hands in clean water, once again dons his ceremonial robes, and returns to the Patriarchate. Along the route he dips a bouquet of flowers in the water that has been used for the footwashing and sprinkles it on the faithful.

60-61 **The Greek-Orthodox Footwashing Ceremony** — It is held in the plaza before the Church of the Holy Sepulchre. (see 59)

62 **The Roman Catholic Procession of the Cross** — "So the soldiers took charge of Jesus. Carrying his own cross he went out to the place of the Skull (which in Aramaic is called Golgotha). Here they crucified him..." (John 19:16-18). The Procession of the Cross is a re-enactment of Jesus' way of the Cross, between his trial at the Praetorium till his crucifixion and burial. The tradition of the Way of the Cross can be traced back to Byzantine times, even though a different route was followed in those days. The route of the present Via Dolorosa dates back to the 13th century, but the final route was determined only in the 19th century.
The Way of the Cross consists of 14 stations, nine of which are found along the Via Dolorosa, while the five remaining ones are inside the Church of the Holy Sepulchre. The location of the stations is based both on descriptions in the New Testament and other, later sources. Next to most of the stations churches were erected. The successive stations are: I. The *Praetorium* (at the site where the Antonia fortress is said to have stood. Today this is the site of the courtyard of the Muslim el-Omariye school); II. The *Flagellation* and *Jesus is made to bear his cross* (Churches of the Flagellation and Judgement); III. *Jesus falls the first time* (the Polish church, which today belongs to the Armenian Catholics); IV. *Jesus meets his sorrowing mother* (the site is located south of the Roman-Catholic Chapel of Mary of the Sorrows); V. *Simon of Cyrene helps Jesus to carry the cross* (a right turn off Haggai Street to the Via Dolorosa, opposite the Franciscan church of Simon of Cyrene); VI. *Veronica wipes Jesus' face* (a pillar in the Greek-Catholic church erected in 1885); VII. *Jesus falls a second time* (a pillar from the Cardo erected in the Via Dolorosa, at the crossing with Beth Habad); VIII. *Jesus speaks to the women of Jerusalem* (a stone engraved with a Maltese cross and the inscription NIKA in a wall further along the way); IX. *Jesus falls a third time* (a pillar from the Cardo, in the wall of a courtyard built on the roof of the Chapel of St. Helena); the stations X to XIV are situated inside the Church of the Holy Sepulchre. (see also 38)

63 **Greek-Orthodox pilgrims cross themselves** — The Greek-Orthodox Procession of the Cross ends at the Church of the Holy Sepulchre. The Patriarch, carrying the cross, ascends the steps leading to the Chapel of the Sorrows, while the faithful remain standing in the plaza to listen to his words. (see also 62)

64 **The procession of the Cross in historical dress** — American pilgrims from San Francisco in contemporary dress re-enact the Way of the Cross. (see also 62)

65 **Yeshiva student in Purim dress** — The Purim festival commemorates the rescue of the Jews from certain destruction during the days of the Persian king Xerxes, as told in the biblical Book of Esther. At Purim the Jews are commanded to read the Book of Esther, to eat, drink and be merry. In order to increase the merriment it is customary for people to dress up. In the Hamatmidim Yeshiva in the Meah She'arim quarter the pupils have exchanged their traditional headgear for a Turkish tarbush. Young boys, who on this day are allowed every kind of liberty, may even smoke cigarettes without fear of censure.

66 **The Latin Patriarch lighting the Holy Fire** — The ceremony, which takes place on the first Saturday of Easter (according to the Gregorian calendar), commemorates the miracle of Jesus' disappearance from the tomb following his burial: "After the Sabbath Mary Magdalena and the other Mary went to look at the tomb, and there was a violent earthquake, for an angel of the Lord came down from heaven... and his appearance was like lightning..." (Matth. 28:1,3). The Patriarch stands in prayer before a censer with burning coals. The Holy Fire is ignited by pouring incense on the coals.

67 **The flame is carried in the Greek-Orthodox ceremony** — The Ceremony of the Holy Fire is the most important of the Easter rites of the Eastern Churches. It takes place on the first Saturday of Easter (according to the Julian calendar).

The most impressive ceremony is the Greek-Orthodox one. At its culmination the Patriarch withdraws inside the Holy Sepulchre, carrying an unlit torch. While the Patriarch prays, it is claimed, a flame descends from Heaven and lights the torch.
Outside the Holy Sepulchre two representatives of the Armenian and Greek Church await the Patriarch's return, each of them holding an unlit torch. Thousands of believers throng the church and the adjoining church plaza carrying special tapers composed of 33 smaller candles — one for each year of Jesus' life on earth. The Patriarch passes the flame through two apertures in the wall of the Holy Sepulchre, enabling the Armenian and Greek prelate to light their torches. These are then used to light the tapers of the faithful, who pass on the flame, until everyone's candle is lit. (see also 66)

68 **Candle lighting during the Roman-Catholic ceremony**. (see 66)

The lights of Jerusalem at night — View of the Old City walls across the Zichron Yosef and Nahlat Ahim Quarters.

69 **Lighting a Jerusalem Hanukkah lamp** — When Judah Maccabee and his brothers entered the Temple following their capture of Jerusalem from the Greeks, they found only one jar of oil pure enough to be used for relighting the Temple candelabrum, sufficient for merely one day. Due to a miracle this one jar lasted eight days — sufficient time to prepare new olive oil. The Feast of Hanukkah commemorates the rededication of the Temple and the miracle of the jar of oil.
During the eight days of the feast Jewish families place a Hanukkah candelabra with lighted candles at their door or window. In the ultra-orthodox areas of Jerusalem a special kind of *hanukkiah* is used. Such a "Jerusalem hanukkiah" is a largish rectangular box with a glass lid, inside which are eight jars of olive oil. After the wicks have been lit the hanukkiah is suspended above the doorway, enabling every passerby to bear witness to the miracle of the oil, while the glass closure protects the flames from wind and rain. The photograph shows a copper hanukkiah crafted by Shlomo Ohana.

70 **The chandelier in the dome of the Catholicon** — The Catholicon of the Church of the Holy Sepulchre is the principal hall of worship at the centre of the basilica. The apse of the Catholicon is roofed with a dome, from which is suspended an enormous chandelier.

71 **Fireworks above the Old City** — Fireworks in celebration of Jerusalem Year.

72-73 **Lag Be'omer celebration at the tomb of Rabbi Simon the Just** — Every year on *Lag Be'omer* ultra-orthodox Jews congregate at the cave tomb of Rabbi Simon the Just to celebrate and to conduct the "halake" ceremony, when three-year old boys receive their first haircut. The celebrants eat, drink and dance, while the children whose hair was cut are showered with sweets. (see also 47)

74 **Street dancers during the launch of Jerusalem Year.** (see 18)

75 **Sweet shabiyat cakes** — an oriental type of confectionery.

76 **The Cardo** — The Cardo was the main thoroughfare of Jerusalem in Roman and Byzantine times. In the course of construction work in the Jewish Quarter of the Old City the ancient road was laid bare along a length of some 150 metres. A colonnade and shops were found on both sides. Several sections of the Cardo have been restored and along one a number of modern shops have been opened. The photograph shows the open part of the Cardo, with a number of the original columns.

77-79 **The Ben-Yehuda Mall** — The lower end of Ben-Yehuda Street and several of the smaller side streets have been repaved and closed to traffic.

80-85 **Market Street** — Scenes from the street market at the Damascus Gate.

86 **Easter eggs** — Easter eggs covered with coloured beads, in imitation of Russian Easter eggs.

87 **The opening ceremonies of Jerusalem Year** — Colourfully dressed groups wend their way marching and dancing through the streets. (see 18)

88 **Lion's Fountain** — The fountain, decorated with copper lions and doves, is situated near the Yemin Moshe quarter.

89 **Corner in an Old City courtyard** — Hens pecking away next to an old waterbasin.

90 **Seats at the Teddy (Kollek) Stadium** — Striking grandstand design by Pasqual and Izzy Broide.

91 **Parking lot near the Damascus Gate**.

92 **A quiet camping place at the Jaffa Gate** — These wooden carts are the principal means of transportation through the Old City alleyways.

93 **Hilton Hotel parking lot at night**.

94-95 **Jewish summer camp closing ceremony at the Western Wall** — During the summer holidays camps are organised in Israel for Jewish youth from abroad. At the conclusion, an impressive night-time ceremony is held at the Western Wall.

96 **Kiryat Wolfson** — residential quarter astride the Sha'arei Hessed quarter, built by Sir Isaac Wolfson opposite the Valley of the Cross and Givat Ram. It consists of five 16-storey towers built atop several layers of terraced villas.

97 **Roof of the Bible Lands Museum** — The museum, a repository of treasures from ancient near-eastern cultures, is situated between the Knesset and the Shrine of the Book. Besides exposition halls, it contains a research library, lecture halls, laboratories, a Hellenistic theatre and an auditorium. The museum was established by Dr. Eli Borowski and his wife Batya.

98-9 **Kiryat Wolfson.** (see 96)

100 **Zion Gate** — Situated west of the southern Old City wall. It provides access to Mount Zion and the Jewish Quarter.
Dung Gate — This gate, situated opposite Silwan (Kfar Shiloah), was named after a gate near the Silwan Pool during Second Temple days. It is the lowest of all gates in the Old City wall; originally it was no more than an opening in one of the watch towers. The Jordanians widened it to allow the passage of vehicles. More recently the gate was widened further and restored.
Golden Gate — This gate, now closed, is situated in the eastern wall of the Haram esh-Sharif, which simultaneously forms a part of the original Old City wall, The gate has two sections, called "Gate of Mercy" and "Gate of Forgiveness" in Hebrew. In Jewish tradition the Messiah will enter through the latter section. According to the Christians Jesus entered Jerusalem through this gate on Palm Sunday. Muslims believe that it will be the site of the Day of Judgement. The gate has been closed ever since the Muslim conquest of Jerusalem from the Crusaders. The slope below the wall contains a Muslim cemetery. The gate appears to have been built during the Ummayad period (8th cent.).
Entrance gate to "City Wall apartments" in Gilo — a residential complex built during the 1970's after a design by Salo Hirschman.

101 **Jaffa Gate** — The only gate in the western section of the Old City wall. It was built during the years 1537-1541 by Sultan Suleiman the Magnificent. During the Byzantine and Crusader periods it was called "Gate of David", after the citadel on its left.

102 **David's Citadel ("Tower of David")** — The present citadel was built during the Middle Ages on the remains of a fortress from the early Arabic era and foundations of towers and walls dating from as far back as the First Temple period, including a high tower built by Herod. The Herodian tower became afterwards known as "David's Tower". During the Jewish monarchy and the Ottoman era the citadel was enlarged. In 1635 the minaret on the citadel was built, which during the 19th century was nicknamed "Tower of David". Today the citadel houses the Museum on the History of Jerusalem.

103 **The Monastery of the Cross** — The monastery is situated in the Valley of the Cross. According to Christian tradition the tree from which the cross of Jesus was made grew here. The monastery was built in the 6th century, in the days of the emperor Justinian. In course of time the monastery was destroyed by the Persians and the Parthians. It was rebuilt during the 11th century by a Georgian monk. During the 17th century the monastery was sold to the Greek-Orthodox Church, who own it till the present day.

104 **Eleona convent** — or "Pater Noster", situated on the Mount of Olives. This is the place where Jesus taught his disciples that the love of God will bring peace to the world. Here stood the 4th-century Byzantine Eleona church (from the Greek for "Mount of Olives"), one of the three most important churches in Palestine. The Crusaders built a chapel on this spot, with the "Lord's Prayer" engraved on one of its walls. The convent which was built between 1872-1889 is occupied by Carmelite nuns.
The Augusta Victoria hospital — The building was erected between 1898-1910 by Augusta Victoria, the wife of the German emperor Wilhelm II, and served as a hospice of the German Templars. Today it is an Arab hospital supported by the World Lutheran Federation.

105 **Hyatt hotel** — This is the largest hotel in Jerusalem, built on the western slope of Mount Scopus. It was opened in 1987 (design: David Reznik and Nitza Raskin).

106-107 **Notre Dame de France** — The building has four floors along a wide front and two wings. The two tall towers in the facade of the church flank a statue of Mary holding the infant Jesus. The complex was built between 1884 and 1904 by a French monastic order. It contains over 400 rooms, including residential quarters, several halls and a church. The building is now owned by the Vatican and operates a youth hostel and a cultural centre.

108 **The bell tower of St. George's cathedral** — The tower stands at the centre of the Anglican church, built at the end of the 19th century. It is a copy of the bell tower of a church in Oxford, and called after the English king Edward VII, who financed its construction.

Minaret of the Sons of A'wanima mosque — The minaret is situated on the north-western corner of the Haram esh-Sharif next to the Antonia (today the Muslim el-Omariye school).

109 **Spice box** — Used during the *havdalah* ceremony at the close of the Jewish Sabbath. This early 18th-century example, created from embossed and incised silver, originates from Germany (artist: J. Rimonim; Stieglitz Collection, Israel Museum). Spice boxes in the shape of a church tower or minaret were quite common in Germany from the late Middle Ages onwards.
Bell tower of the Mar Zakariya church — in the Russian Mar Zakariya monastery in Ein Karem. The Arabs call the church "el-Muscovia" after the Russian capital.

110 **Church of the Redeemer** — A German-Lutheran church built on the foundations of the Crusader church of Sancta Maria Latina, erected with donations from businessmen of the Italian town of Amalfi. The Lutheran church was dedicated in 1898 by the German emperor Wilhelm II during his visit to Jerusalem.

111 **Church of the Visitation** — This Franciscan church in Ein Karem dates from 1955 (design: Barluzzi). One wall of the church courtyard is decorated with 45 glazed tiles containing the Magnificat prayer in as many languages. The Magnificat is the song of praise uttered by Mary during her visit to the home of Elizabeth and Zechariah, the parents of John the Baptist, on the traditional site of which the church is built.

112-113 **View of Jerusalem from Mount Scopus** — Mount Scopus is the northern extension of the ridge of which the Mount of Olives forms the centre. Its highest point lies at 829 metres above sea level.

114 **Mount Scopus and the Hebrew University in the snow** — In 1913 the World Zionist Organization purchased a tract of land at the top of Mount Scopus, and in 1918 the corner stone of the Hebrew University was laid here. The university was opened on April 1st, 1925 with a festive ceremony. During its initial year it had 164 students in three faculties: Jewish studies, chemistry and biology. In course of time dozens of other faculties and numerous buildings were added. In 1948 Mount Scopus was cut off from Jewish Jerusalem, to remain a Jewish enclave within Jordan territory. The various faculties were transferred to other buildings in Jerusalem itself, and eventually concentrated in a new campus at Givat Ram.
Following the reunification of the city the Mount Scopus campus was restored and many of the faculties were returned there.

115 **The Mormon University** — The university, situated along the slope of Mount Scopus, is an annex of Brigham Young Mormon university in the United States.

116 **The Wohl Torah Center** — The site of Yeshivat Hakotel in the Jewish quarter of the Old City. The building, designed by Eliezer Frankel, was inaugurated in 1987. It also houses a museum containing archaeological finds unearthed during the construction.

117 **Hebrew Union College** — The faculty of Jewish studies of the American Progressive (Reform) movement. The college has departments of Bible studies and archeology, as well as a rabbinical school.

118-119 **The Israel Museum** — Israel's national museum, established in 1965 on the southern hill of the Givat Ram ridge. The museum has four sections: art, including a sculpture garden, the Bronfman archaeological museum, the Shrine of the Book, and the Youth Wing. The complex consists of a series of interlocking buildings (architects: Dora Gad and Eli Mansfeld). The Shrine of the Book houses the Dead Sea scrolls, biblical manuscripts and other archaeological finds from the Judean desert. The white dome, built in the shape of the lid of a jar in which the ancient scrolls were placed, symbolizes the sect of the Sons of Light.

120 **Islamic Museum** — The museum, devoted to Islamic art, contains archives, libraries and an exhibition of Islamic art. The building, which was inaugurated in 1975, has a vaulted facade with pillars of reddish-brown stone.

121 **The Rockefeller Museum** — Archaeological museum established between 1930-1938 by the British Mandatory government with funds donated by the American Rockefeller family. The museum is located in Suleiman Street, opposite the Old City wall.

122-123 **The Hadassa hospital at Ein-Karem** — The

Hadassa Medical Center in Ein-Karem was inaugurated in 1961. The hospital complex also includes a medical school, dental, pharmaceutical and psychiatric faculties, as well a synagogue, with Marc Chagall's famous stained glass windows.

124-125 **The Italian hospital and the Department of Education building** — The hospital was founded between 1912 and 1919 as a convent by an Italian monastic order (design: A. Barluzzi). Outstanding features of the building, erected in Tuscan Renaissance style, are the square bell tower, the octagonal church and the crenellated walls of the main building. Following World War I the building was converted into a hospital. During World War II it served as headquarters of the British Royal Air Force and as a military hospital. After the establishment of the State of Israel the building was returned to its original owners. In 1963 it was sold to the State, and since then houses part of the Ministry of Eduction and Culture. The church was restored and is now used as a conference and lecture hall.

126 **The Dome of the Rock.** (see 16, 128)

127 **The Haram esh-Sharif at night.** (see 16)

128 **The Abyssinian Church** — This circular church is topped by a black dome crowned with an Abyssinian cross — a cross within a circle, from which radiate seven arrows. The church was built at the end of the 19th century by the Abyssinian emperors John IV and Menelik II. The outer wall of the church facade encloses two circular galleries. The central part, which forms the sanctuary, contains the altar built according to the description of the altar in the Second temple.
Dome of the Rock (the Golden Dome) — The central edifice of the Haram esh-Sharif, built over *Es-Sakhra,* the "Foundation Stone". The edifice, erected by the Umma-yad caliph Abd el-Malik in the year 691, is one of the finest and most famous examples of early Islamic art.
The building is octagonal in shape and covered with a dome supported by a drum. It is clad with slabs of marble and glazed tiles of Turkish manufacture, which were brought here during the 16th century by Suleiman the Magnificent. During the Jordanian period the dome was covered with gold-anodised aluminium sheets, which explains the name "Golden Dome'. The radius of the dome is identical to that of the Church of the Holy Sepulchre. The structure has four entrances, the western one being the present main entrance. The splendid facade is richly decorated. (see also 16)
Sabil Qaitbay — A Mamluk drinking fountain on the Haram esh-Sharif, located before the western stairs leading to the central platform. It is a square stone edifice measuring 5 by 5 metres. The structure is surmounted by an octagonal drum, crowned with a dome decorated with plant reliefs. Its height is 14 metres and it is called after Quaitbay, who renovated it in the year 1482.
"Yeled tov Jerushala'im" ("A good Jerusalem boy") — A motto frequently embroidered on children's headcoverings, which in course of time became a phrase indicating someone who does everything in a proper way.

129 **Church of the Holy Sepulchre. Domes of the rotunda and the Catholicon** — The large dome overarches the cupola above the Holy Sepulchre. The dome was built in the course of restorations following a big conflagration in the church. Till then the rotunda had been capped by a truncated dome, the top of which was open to the sky. The smaller dome belongs to the Catholicon, the hall of worship at the central part of the church. The dome was erected during the Crusader era. (see 38)

130 **The Russian Ascension Church** — The church is situated on the Mount of Olives. According to Christian tradition this is the spot where Jesus ascended to heaven. The spot of the Ascension is marked by a round stone embedded in the courtyard. The church, which was built between the years 1870-1887, belongs to the White Russian Church. In front of the church stands a 30-metre high square bell tower.

131 **Church of the Sisters of the Rosary convent** — Part of the convent of the Sisters of the Rosary, a Catholic order founded in Nazareth by a Christian Arab, which is mainly engaged in education.
St. Peter in Gallicantu church — A church on Mount Zion, called after St. Peter, who denied Jesus three times before the cock crowed. It is built on Byzantine and Crusader church foundations.
The Florence Dworsky Conservatory — Situated in the botanical garden of the Hebrew University's Givat Ram campus.
The Dominus Flevit church — *Dominus flevit* is Latin for "the Lord weeps". The cupola of the church is shaped like a teardrop, to commemorate Jesus' weeping for Jerusalem (Luke 19:41-44). The church was built by the Franciscans in 1954-1955 (design: A. Barluzzi) on the remains of a Byzantine church.

132 **Mount of Olives. View from the east** — The Mount of Olives lies at the centre of a ridge running from north to south. Its highest point is 815 metres above sea level. According to Jewish tradition the Divine presence continued to rest on the mountain following the destruction of the Temple, and Jews used to ascend it in order to gaze upon the Temple Mount. In Christian tradition the mount is connected with the events during Jesus' final days on earth. Here he taught his disciples, here he awaited his capturers, and from here he ascended to heaven after rising from the dead. Many important churches were built on the mountain. On the brow of the hill lies the Arab village of A-Tur.

133 **The Jewish cemetery on the Mount of Olives** — From the end of the 15th century onwards Jews began to bury their dead at the southern slope of the Mount of Olives, near the Tomb of Zachariah. According to popular belief the resurrection of the dead will begin at the Mount of Olives. The cemetery contains some 70,000 tombs.

134 **Absalom's Tomb** — A monumental tomb on the lower slope of the Mount of Olives. Tradition has it that it was built by Absalom, the rebellious son of king David, based on the words of 2 Samuel 18:18: "During his lifetime Absalom had taken a pillar and erected it in the King's Valley as a monument to himself, for he thought: 'I have no son to carry on the memory of my name.' He named the pillar after himself and it is called Absalom's monument to this day." Its location does not correspond to the Biblical description. Archaeologists date the monument to around the 1st century A.D.

135 **Golden cupolas of the Church of Mary Magdalene** — A church and monastery of the White Russian Church. The church, which was built by Czar Alexander III during the years 1885-1888, is dedicated to Maria Magdalena, after whom his mother Maria Alexandrova was also named.

136-137 **The Russian Cathedral** — The church, situated in the Russian Compound, was erected between 1860 and 1872. It is built of white stone and has eight green domes. The basilica is built in typical Russian-Orthodox style. The large central dome is surrounded by four smaller domes. Two more domes crown the bell towers in the facade, while there is an additional small dome atop the central aisle. The bells, which were brought from Russia in 1856, were the first bells in Jerusalem, since the Ottoman authorities had never permitted the ringing of church bells in the city.

138 **Mount Zion** — This hill, situated at 765 metres above sea level, rises south of the Old City wall overlooking the western heights. Even though situated outside the Old City proper, it is considered an integral part of it, both topographically and because of its important role throughout the city's history. According to Jewish and Islamic tradition king David was buried on Mount Zion. Adjoining the traditional

David's Tomb is an underground Holocaust memorial room. On the mount are situated the Church of the Dormition and the Coenaculum, the traditional room of the Last Supper, as well as other churches and monasteries.

139 **The Stepped Structure in the City of David** — Remnants of the foundations of the palace of king David, a man-made mound dating from late-Canaanite times (14th-13th cent. B.C.), constructed from stone embankments filled with a mixture of earth and rubble. It would appear that the ancient acropolis of Canaanite Jerusalem stood on this mound. King David strengthened the mound, adding a stepped buttressing wall before erecting his palace. The structure is situated at the north-eastern corner of the excavations in the City of David.

140 **Mount Zion hotel** — Situated above the Hinnom Valley, opposite Mount Zion. It was built in 1892 as St. John's Ophthalmic Hospital and abandoned in 1948. In 1986, following renovations, the building opened as a hotel.

141 **Haceldama** — According to Christian tradition this site, situated in the Hinnom Valley, was the "field of blood" purchased by the priests with the thirty pieces of silver that Judas Iscariot returned. A Greek-Orthodox monastery was founded here in 1892. The monastery stands on an underground cave from the Second Temple period.

142 **The Palace building** — Formerly the Palace Hotel, built between 1927-1929 by the Islamic *Waqf*. It is situated at the corner of Agron and David Ben-Shimon streets, and presently houses the Ministry of Commerce and Industry.

143 **Terra Sancta college** — Situated at the corner of Keren Hayesod and Ben-Maimon streets (design: A. Barluzzi). It was built by the Franciscan Order and inaugurated in 1927. At present it contains a church and residential quarters for monks, besides which the complex houses several departments of the Hebrew University.

144 **Reflections in the windows of the Hyatt hotel.** (see 105)

145 **Sheraton-Plaza hotel** — This hotel, with 22 floors, rises at the junction of King George Street and Independence Park (design: Mordehai Ben-Horin). It was completed in 1974.

146 **The Jerusalem Theatre. The Henry Crown Concert Hall** — The Jerusalem Theatre complex includes the Sherover Theatre (in the older part, inaugurated in 1971), the Henry Crown concert hall, the Rebecca Crown auditorium, and the small hall, all of which were inaugurated in 1986. In addition there are a restaurant and a bookshop.

147 **Kennedy Memorial** — Erected in 1966 in memory of President Kennedy with money donated by American Jews. The building stands on the top of a hill at 842 metres above sea level, and built in the shape of a sawn off tree trunk (design: Dov Feigin).

148-149 **The Jewish Quarter and the Temple Mount in the snow**.

150 **Dawn above the Jewish Quarter**.

151 **A rosy sunrise above the Old City**.

152 **The Christian Quarter bathed in sunshine** — The Christian Quarter occupies the north-western part of the Old City. It owes its name to the presence of more than thirty Christian religious institutions. At its centre stands the Church of the Holy Sepulchre, the holiest place in Christendom. (see also 2)

153 **Coral sunset on the Zichron Yosef Quarter** — This neighbourhood, situated south of the Mahane Yehuda market, was built in 1931.

154 **Batei Ungarn** — This complex, with a large interior courtyard, was established during the final decade of the 19th century to accommodate Jews from Austria, Hungary and Bohemia. The first houses were occupied in 1901. Its residents are ultra-orthodox Jews.

155 **Yemin Moshe Quarter** — This neighborhood was established in 1892 by the Montefiore Foundation. Its 130 residences were to be shared equally between Ashkenazi and Sephardi Jewish families. In 1967 the site was taken over by the Jerusalem municipality. The houses and streets were renovated while maintaining their original style. At present it is regarded as one the most prestigious neighbourhoods of the city.

156 **The Ramot Polin Quarter** — This residential neighbourhood straddles the eastern Ramot ridge. It owns its fame to its unique architectural style: multi-faceted houses constructed from pre-fabricated elements.

157 **Tin-clad walls in Mahane Yehuda** — Several of the old apartment buildings have been covered with sheets of tinplate against penetration of rain water.

158 **Laromme hotel** — The hotel, overlooking the Liberty Bell Gardens, is built around a large central courtyard. The building slopes towards the adjoining valley. The hotel was completed in 1982 (design: Yaacov Rechter).

159 **The convent of the Franciscan Sisters** — Built in 1936 by the Franciscan Missionary Sisters of the Immaculate Heart of Mary, it serves as a school and orphanage.

160 **Silwan (Kfar Shiloah)** — This Arab village lies along the slope of the Mount of Corruption (2 Kings 23:13), on the southern part of the Mount of Olives. Silwan, the Arab name of the village, is a corruption of the name Siloam mentioned in the New Testament, which in turn was derived from the Hebrew name Shiloah.

161 **The Gilo Quarter** — Gilo was built during the 1970's south of Jerusalem, between Beth Safafa and Bethlehem. The neighbourhood is characterised by its rich architectural diversity.

162 **Stairway in Yemin Moshe.** (see 155)

163 **Haas Promenade** — Situated between north Talpioth and the wooded grounds surrounding the former High Commissioner's residence. It is 800 metres long and includes an observation plaza. The promenade was built between 1982 and 1987 with funds donated by the Haas family.

164 **The Garden of Gethsemane and the Church of All Nations** — The garden is located at the foot of the Mount of Olives, along the Jerusalem-Jericho road. According to Christian tradition this was the olive grove to which Jesus and his disciples retired after the Last Supper, and where he bade farewell to all but three of his disciples — Petrus, James and John. To this place Judas Iscariot guided the Roman soldiers who came to arrest him. The Church of All Nations was erected during 1919-1924 (design: A. Barluzzi) on the remains of Byzantine and Crusader churches, with donations from Catholics all over the world — which explains its name. Adjoining the church is a Franciscan monastery.

The Garden Tomb — Anglican Christians point to a burial cave with two rooms on this spot as the burial place of Jesus. The cave is carved in a rock whose shape suggests a skull. In 1882 the British general Charles Gordon identified this rock as Golgotha (from the Hebrew *gulgolet* = skull). The burial cave was discovered by the German archaeologist Conrad Schick. The site is maintained by the Anglican Church.

165 **Sherover Promenade** — The promenade, named after Gabriel Sherover, lies on the slope below the Haas Promenade. It was opened in 1989.

166 **Adventure playground** — The playground is situated below the Sherover Promenade.

167 **Apartment buildings in Givat Oren and Givat Haporetsim** — These neighbourhoods were built during the 1950's in the southern part of the city.

168 **The swimming pool of the King David Hotel** — This hotel, situated in King David Street, was built in 1930 and it is one of the oldest and most luxurious in the city.

169 **Bethesda Pool (Sheep Pool)** — The pool, which was uncovered during excavations next to St. Anne's church, is identified with the Sheep Pool from the Second Temple period and the Bethesda Pool in the New Testament. The pool, built in Hasmonean times, covers an area of 150x50 metres. Its two reservoirs are 15 metres deep. In it was collected the water from the Bethsaida stream. During the Byzantine era a church was erected on top of the wall separating the two sections of the pool. Remains of the church and the supporting columns are visible in the photograph.
The swimming pool of the American Colony hotel — The hotel, situated in St. George's Street, originally was the residence of a rich Arab. About 100 years ago the villa was sold to a group of Swedish-American settlers led by Anna Spafford from Chicago. Today the building is used as a hotel.
The Jerusalem pool — Located at Emek Refa'im, this was the first swimming pool in Jerusalem.
The Mamilla Pool in the snow — An ancient reservoir used for collecting rainwater.

170 **Yad Vashem** — Yad Vashem, situated on Remembrance Hill, is the national Holocaust memorial. The site houses a research and documentation centre, museums, a remembrance hall and a synagogue. The surrounding grounds contain various commemoration sites and monuments.

171 **President's residence** — This is the official residence of the Presidents of Israel. It was inaugurated in 1971 (design: A. Elchanani). The building includes the President's offices, a reception hall and residential quarters. The building in the lower part of the photograph is a synagogue and community centre.

172 **Hechal Shelomo** — The seat of the Chief Rabbinate of Israel, built between 1953-1958. It contains the offices of the Chief Rabbinate, the Rabbinical Court, a religious library, a museum, various halls and a synagogue, whose furniture was brought here from an old synagogue in Padua, Italy.

173 **The Knesset covered in snow** — The Knesset is the seat of the Israeli legislature. The building, whose construction was financed by the James de Rothschild family (design: Klarwein), was inaugurated on August 30, 1966.

174 **Ruins of the "Hurva" synagogue** — Officially the Beth Yaacov synagogue, named after Baron Jacob (James) de Rothschild. Ashkenazi Jewish life was once centred in this area around a synagogue dating from 1705. In 1721 the Ashkenazi residential quarter and the synagogue were destroyed. Between 1856-1864 the new synagogue was built on its ruins, that are commemorated in the synagogue's pseudonym "Hurva" (= ruin). The new synagogue, which rose to a height of 25 metres, was the highest building in the Jewish quarter. It formed the centre of Jewish life in Palestine.
In 1948 Jordanian soldiers blew up the synagogue. Following the Six-Day War one arch of the building was re-erected as a memorial.

175 **The Jewish Quarter** — The Jewish Quarter is situated in the south-eastern part of the Old City. It is bounded by the Western Wall in the east, the Old City wall in the west, the Street of the Chain to the north and the Armenian quarter to the south. During the 15th century the Jewish community of Jerusalem moved from Mount Zion to a new location within the walls, which would be their home for the next 550 years, until 1948 and the occupation of the Jewish quarter by the Jordanian army. Most of the quarter, in particular its many synagogues, were destroyed by the Jordanians. Following the reunification of the city after the Six-Day War, parts of the quarter were rebuilt.

176 **Section of the excavations at the Western Wall** — At the right are the steps to the Huldah Gates. The photograph shows remains of the 8th century Ummayad palace that remained unfinished, as well as of other buildings.

177 **Section of the Jewish Quarter** — The outlines of the roofs show a striking similarity to the ground plan of the buildings that were unearthed during excavations near the Western Wall.

178 **The Archaeological Garden and the rebuilt Jewish Quarter** — Archaeological excavations and [part of] the ancient Jewish quarter which was destroyed and rebuilt a number of times. (see also 175)

179 **Remains of the Ummayad palace and the el-Aqsa mosque** — The palaces of the Ummayads and the el-Aqsa mosque were built during the same period on the ruins of earlier structures. The palaces were destroyed, but the mosque has survived until today. (see also 43, 176)

180 **Roof of the President's residence.** (see 171)
Baklava — Sweet oriental cakes made of layers of pastry with nuts an honey.
Patio at the Hilton hotel — The hotel, built in 1972, is situated at the entrance to Jerusalem (design: Yaacov Rechter).
Swimming pool at the Laromme hotel. (see 158)

181 **Honeycomb apartments at Ramot Polin.** (see 156)
"Center 1" Shopping Mall — A shopping mall at the entrance to Jerusalem.
Farewell ! — A green farewell greeting at the exit of the city.
Welcome ! — "We welcome the messiah." An eager salutation on a rooftop on the Mount of Olives.

182-183 **Sunset** — The sun setting over the Old City.